Winter

Celebrating the Season in a Christian Home

Peter Mazar

LTP

Liturgy Training Publications

ACKNOWLEDGMENTS

Winter, copyright © 1996, Archdiocese
of Chicago: Liturgy Training Publications,
1800 North Hermitage Avenue, Chicago IL
60622-1101; 1-800-933-1800;
FAX1-800-933-7094. All rights reserved.

This book was produced as a collaboration
between the author, Peter Mazar; the designer,
M. Urgo and the editor, Gabe Huck. Mary Jo
Huck assisted in the early stages of planning for
the design. Illustrations are by Judy Jarrett,
electronic graphics are by M. Urgo. Unless
otherwise noted, photos are from Digital Stock
Corporation. Production by M. Urgo and Mark
Hollopeter with assistance from D. Kulov and
Kari Nicholls. The typefaces used are Futura,
New Baskerville, and Dolmen. Printing was by
Worzalla, Stevens Point, Wisconsin.

Library of Congress Catalog Card Number
96-077353
ISBN 1-56854-134-1
WINTER

Contents

Passing Over into Winter

When it first appears on the scene, winter is greeted graciously, even jubilantly. We call it "brisk" and "invigorating." We sing the praises of the first frost, the first snow. Jingle all the way! But the weeks go by, and those damp, gray days keep coming.

Sometimes the only way around things is straight through them, so some of us make the most of winter sports. Others immerse themselves more deeply in work or hobbies or volunteer efforts, in community theater or a chorale, in good reading and good music — listening to it and making it. Still others take pleasure in the simple joys of the season, such as fixing a big pot of soup.

But eventually, for many of us, winter overstays its welcome. Enough already! We want winter to end. For some people, the short days bring on serious depression. They need light. We all need light.

Of course, people have been enduring winter, and enjoying it too, for many generations.

A wealth of human traditions has evolved for making the most of the season. Many of these humane and sensible and healthful traditions have shaped and have been shaped by the Christian calendar. They have become part of the Christian way of life.

This small book is an exploration of some of these customs — things like trees and gift-giving. We'll look at what makes them light-bearing. And we'll also look at what makes them Christian.

Our winter begins with the time called Advent, really the tail end of autumn. During Advent in the Northern Hemisphere the days grow as short as they get. The coming of winter

brings with it a mix of enthusiasm and dread. Those are good words to describe Advent.

Advent requires waiting for Christmas. The waiting can be hard, but keeping Advent is worth a struggle. We don't want to lose a time that so powerfully and mystically tells us who we are and who we need to become. Advent is part of our Christian identity.

Advent gets us to the winter solstice, the longest night of the year. After

the solstice, days begin to grow longer. Christians latch onto this tiny sign of hope and make it the occasion of a magnificent "passing over" festival. We know our whole lives are a "passing over" into Christ, but what a name this festival gets! We call it "Christmas," "Christ's Mass," "Christ's worshipful celebration." Ponder that name.

The season of Christmas lasts from Christmas Day until

the feast of the Baptism of the Lord, well into January. This merry season begins with the "twelve days of Christmas" and reaches its high point at Epiphany, Twelfth Night. Forty days after Christmas the church has a day for one last echo of the season: February 2, Candlemas, when we celebrate the meeting with two elderly prophets, Simeon and Anna. Old age embraces youth, and Christmas itself "departs in peace."

But then comes Carnival time, which gets us cheerfully to Lent and Winter's end.

Advent, Christmas and Carnival are the church's winter. This approach to the season is meant to be healthy

for the soul: first the waiting, then the celebrating, and then even some excess to get ourselves in gear for the hard work of a new spring. Winter blesses the land with rest and renewal. It can bless us as well with genuine recreation—which "creates us anew."

The season of Advent begins four Sundays before Christmas Day. But like any season, Advent announces itself weeks earlier. Throughout the autumn we slip and slide gradually into Advent, like leaves falling off a tree until at last the tree is bare, or like snowflakes falling one by one until the landscape is buried.

"Advent" is the name we've given to the last and most intense stage in a process that's been unfolding for several months, as nights lengthen and the cold intensifies.

During Advent our tradition is to keep things plain and untinseled. We take our cue from nature, where a simplicity sets in after the harvest, where autumn's glory has been muted and made fallow. When Advent is completed, Christmas will bring plenty of occasions for lights and greenery and feasting, but for now we settle into winter and learn its marvelous lessons.

This isn't an exercise in browbeating. A season of silence attunes the ear to hear angel songs. A season of darkness adapts the eye to see once again that star of wonder.

At this time of year the church pays extra heed to Israel's prophets. They spoke to a people

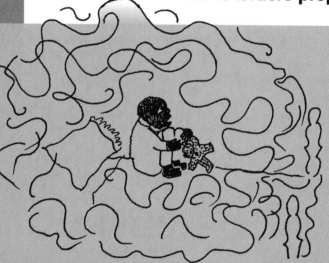

For some of our ancestors the completion of the harvest brought with it the year's rarest resource—free time! Winter was the most likely season for singing, dancing and storytelling, for repairing what got broken and for creating something new. Winter, with its free time, is the original "holiday season."

The winter festivals are more than an excuse for some fun. They can be a matter of life or death. In the old days, the winter festivals were a necessary antidote for one of the crippling sicknesses of the season—fear. What if mice get into the corncrib? What if the firewood runs out? What if the baby's cough doesn't clear up?

Today winter usually is far less fearful than in the past. Most of us can count on heat, food, transportation, and a dose of antibiotics. But without these things in ample supply, the old fears return. Winter underscores our dependence on one another. An Irish sea chantey shouts it lustily:

So it's all right, Jock, as we sing this song,
for the days are cold and the nights are long!
Let's all join hands and form a chain
    'til the leaves of springtime bloom again.

at risk of being crippled by their fears, of lapsing into despair, of being overwhelmed by the work required to fix problems. Isaiah, Jeremiah, Mary, John the Baptist and Jesus together announce the coming of God's reign of justice. (And coming is what "advent" means.) That reign, so they say, will be like a wedding, like a path through the wilderness, like the consolation of the grieving, like a homecoming, like the birth of a child.

Many seasonal customs have their origins in the practical necessities of winter.
Christians claim that the essential things, the things that matter most, can be windows into God's reign. And so at this season we try to name and face our fears and our deepest needs.

One such necessary wintertime task was the storage of seed for next year's crops. God forbid that anything or anyone should consume it! The seed often took the form of a sheaf of grain hung in a corner, which sometimes was called "grandmother" and got the loving respect the name implies. In many places, straw and grain — more than evergreens — are signs of the season.

Because this custom has to do with safeguarding a harvest for future generations, an expression of it today might be to make sure that as many people as possible have a share in the bounty of the harvest.

Winter is a natural season to keep filling an "almsbox" or other container for money and gifts for those in need. And winter offers ample opportunities for some first-hand involvement in long-term or immediate help to people in need. The parish office probably has a list of phone numbers for anyone willing. (Or see page 29.)

Back in the days before modern paving, travel often was impossible during winter.
Dirt roads got rutted with ice or choked with mud, making wheels useless. Imagine what it was like to say goodbye to people in autumn whom you wouldn't be able to visit again until spring. Imagine also what it's like to be forced by the weather to stay at home

in the company of your household. This really is the time for good will to everyone.

The custom of the Advent wreath probably has its origins in this annual impediment to travel. In some climates at the onset of winter, after the year's farm work was mostly finished, wagon wheels would sometimes be brought indoors and hung high to keep them from warping. Maybe Christians got to thinking how the suspended wheels make fine signs of the season, a season that in some places was called Yule, a word related to "wheel," a good word for the turning of the year.

Let's decorate our wheels with fragrant evergreens and shining candles! Let's light more and more lamps as the nights grow ever longer! In the words of an Austrian rhyme:

**First one, then two, then three, then four —
And then the Christ knocks on the door!**

The four candles of an Advent wreath or the 24 windows of an Advent calendar aren't really a countdown to Christmas. If anything, they're a "count up." As the days and weeks of Advent go by, we light more lights, we open more doors, hope upon hope, until at Christmas we have made for ourselves a festival of wholeness, perfection and fulfillment.

Naturally, there are all sorts of seasonal customs involving fire and light. It's a fairly widespread winter custom to bless the hearth and to honor the all-important stack of firewood with special ceremonies. One ceremony involved trying to keep a single enormous log burning through the Twelve Days of Christmas. While this "yule log" burned, no work or squabbling was allowed.

To keep the spirit of this custom, bless the Lord for your furnace and stove and for the fuel that keeps them going. Help someone in need to pay a fuel bill. Light a small candle each night and refuse to do anything even resembling work as long as it burns. Declare a kind of family truce whenever you light your Advent wreath or Christmas tree.

As the old year wanes and a new one is born, many people still make an effort to live the way they want to live all year long. Look how the practical — the need for light and warmth — leads to the super practical — getting along with each other, savoring peace.

Hymnus.

IV **C** Ondi-tor alme sí-de-rum, Ætérna lux cre-dénti- um,

Christe Redémptor ómni- um, Exáudi pre-ces súppli-cum.

Every autumn the church begins to think about the coming of Judgment Day. Come December and Advent, the church is still thinking about the end of all things, and with mixed feelings. Here's an Advent song that has something of these "end times" to it:

Dear Maker of the stars of night,
Your people's everlasting light,
O Christ, Redeemer of us all,
We pray you hear us when we call.

In sorrow that the ancient curse
Should doom to death a universe,
You came, O Savior, to set free
Your own in glorious liberty.

Come, Sun and Savior, to embrace
Our gloomy world, its weary race,
As groom to bride, as bride to groom:
The wedding chamber, Mary's womb!

This is an English translation of a favorite Advent carol from the Middle Ages, *"Conditor alme siderum."* It's a song to learn by heart. Once that's accomplished, you can sing it outdoors at night under a starry sky. The steam of your breath can rise as a kind of incense to carry your prayer to heaven.

For an Advent wreath, you can use a sturdy, "double-faced" evergreen wreath (one that looks good on both sides). That kind of wreath doesn't curl much when it dries. Or use a pine cone wreath and fix it up with fresh evergreen twigs.

You can put the wreath flat on a table, but the old tradition is to hang it. It's wonderful to gaze up into an Advent wreath, like a hole to peek into heaven!

As hangers, four ribbons might work, but most ribbons tear easily. Long strips of fabric or even chain will do the trick. Use wire to attach each strip or chain to the wreath and then bundle all four together with wire. Hang it from a hook in the ceiling or from a securely anchored ceiling light. If you do this, of course, the wreath can't be hung so high that its candles scorch the ceiling!

Some card stores sell Advent candle holders. Basically they are candle holders with a wire sticking out the bottom. The nail nestles down into the branches and keeps the candle straight. Many central Europeans use red candles, but other people use candles that match their parish's vestment colors, and some folks use glass-enclosed votive candles.

Another tradition is to hang the wreath at the spot where the Christmas tree will go. When the tree finally arrives, the wreath can stay as a kind of crown that tops the tree. Advent's four lights prepare us for the countless lights of Christmas.

No matter where the wreath goes, the most important tradition is to have one and to use it. Light the candles each evening and offer your prayer and song by their increasing light.

> *O Savior, rend the heavens wide!*
> *Come down, come down with mighty stride.*
> *Unlock the gates, the doors break down;*
> *Unbar the way to heaven's crown!*
>
> *Come, Child of God! Without your light*
> *We grope in dread and gloom of night.*
> *Come lead us with a gentle hand*
> *From exile to the promised land.*

This is from a wonderful old Advent carol by Friedrich von Spee, based on words of the prophet Isaiah. The carol can be sung to its own glorious melody or to the tune for "Praise God from whom all blessings flow."

In That Great Gettín' Up Morning!

The good bishop, Nicholas. Our Advent anticipation of the "end times" are woven for us not only in the scriptures and songs at worship but even in customs and folklore. Our fun and games can bolster our faith.

Let's take a look at Saint Nicholas Day, December 6. Doom's Day and the Advent feast of Bishop Nicholas are not too strange a pair!

For the moment, put aside any thoughts of Santa Claus. Santa keeps tabs on who's naughty or nice, but Bishop Nicholas stares straight into the face of human sinfulness. Santa brings dreams of sugarplums, but Nicholas is a Wheaties kind of guy. Even his name means "champion."

> Let us know each fault and failing,
> We will bear your harshest railing.
> Welcome, Bishop, so we sing:
> Tell us, tell us everything!
> —from a Dutch carol

According to the old traditions, Nicholas isn't jolly. He's noble, stern and even curmudgeonly as he marches into a home on his feast day to give every member, not gifts but a tongue-lashing. And as a double dose of reproach, the bishop's devil-like companion threatens the unrepentant with fire and brimstone, no doubt having learned manners from John the Baptist, another of Advent's grouchy saints.

Parents who nowadays would like to organize such a traditional visit from Saint Nicholas might balk at its scariness (although it's hardly scarier than Halloween). The good old customs have us facing our troubles, not sugarcoating them.

All in all, a visit from Saint Nicholas is a wonderful experience—when you finally see the back of him. That's when the treats arrive as a kind of booby prize for sinners. The good news is that we've gotten off with a warning—this time. Next time—and the time is rapidly approaching, so Advent insists—it will be our Lord and Judge knocking on the door, not his deputy.

Do you know someone willing to put on Nicholas's miter (the pointed bishop's hat), to bear his crosier (the shepherd's crook) and to pay your home a visit? It doesn't take much more than donning a cardboard hat, a broom-handle crook, and perhaps a ring and a robe to step into the holy bishop's shoes for the night. You yourself might be

fortified by his awesome presence to walk your own street for the benefit of your neighbors.

In some places Nicholas never appears directly but instead leaves surprising evidence of his blessings, perhaps secretly in someone's shoes during the night or on someone's doorstep or on the handle of someone's office door.

The bishop's gifts are small and simple and yet rich in meaning. Candy canes are sweet emblems of his crosier. Tangerines represent the gold he once gave to a poor family to prevent the daughters from being sold into slavery. Gingerbread and Smyrna figs can remind us of his diocese in what is now Turkey along the spice routes where Asia, Africa and Europe meet.

Oh, yes, and there are those other two tokens that Nicholas carries along in case of dire need—switches and coal! If you're ever the recipient, bear in mind that they make a cozy fire, a lovely place to curl up and read the legends or to listen to Benjamin Britten's marvelous oratorio (Hyperion Records, CDA66333) about this beloved fourth-century bishop.

On Saint Lucy's Day you, too, can welcome the bride to your home. To do that simply, the first to waken serves everyone breakfast in bed. That's rehearsal for resurrection day!

In some places folks serve saffron-colored pastries baked in circles and swirls as ancient tokens of the coming solstice. These are called "Lucy cats" because the twisting shapes resemble cats' tails. Spiral cinnamon rolls or even doughnuts will do just fine as emblems of eternity.

To enrich this ceremony, the breakfast-bringer can dress in a gown, carry candles, wear a ringlet of evergreen on the head, or go all out and wear the traditional crown of seven candles. The most charming aspect of Lucy's Day is an eye-opening blaze of candlelight before dawn. Even on a busy day there's a moment of enchantment. All of Advent brings the easiest time of year for rising before sunrise and for giving thanks to God by dawn's early light.

A week later, on December 13, Saint Lucy arrives with her own warnings. She's like one of the wise bridesmaids of the 25th chapter of Matthew's gospel. They too had no patience with the foolish. Keep your lamps burning, says the martyr Lucy, whose name means "light."

The long, long darkness can attune the eye to a new kind of mystical illumination. In the words of a Swedish hymn:

O Lucy bride, your day of light
awakens sleepy eyes.
Soon will a better dawn make bright
the path to paradise.

Have you ever seen "Saint Lucy's stars"? Another name for them is the Geminid meteor shower, because the "shooting stars" seem to radiate from the constellation Gemini, about one every few minutes. Before dawn on December 12 and 13 is the best time to see the meteors. They can remind us of Jesus' words about the falling stars that will herald the last days (Matthew 24:29).

Advent is the right season for stargazing, for growing accustomed to the night, for searching for light, however fleeting or faint, shining in the darkness.

What's It to Be, Advent or "the Holidays"?

THE
COMMERCIAL
CALENDAR

ONLY 15 MORE
SHOPPING DAYS
TO CHRISTMAS

DEC. 10
DEC. 11
DEC. 12
DEC. 13
DEC. 14
DEC. 15
DEC. 16
DEC. 17
DEC. 18
DEC. 19
DEC. 20
DEC. 21
DEC. 22
DEC. 23
DEC. 24

CHRISTMAS!

CHRISTMAS GIFT
RETURNS

DEC. 26
DEC. 27
DEC. 28
DEC. 29

NEW YEARS EVE!

POST CHRISTMAS
SALES

JAN. 1
JAN. 2
JAN. 3
JAN. 4
JAN. 5
JAN. 6
JAN. 7
JAN. 8
JAN. 9
JAN.10

Maybe the first thing we can do to get ready for Christmas is to ask the hard questions — ourselves, with family or with friends: Why do we keep this festival? What are we celebrating?

Here's another hard question: Which calendar will we follow — our church's calendar with its seasons of Advent and then Christmastime, or the commercial calendar with its "holiday season"?

Can't we keep both calendars? After all, we need to keep all sorts of calendars in balance: work calendars, family calendars, social calendars, academic calendars.

The trouble is that the church's calendar and the commercial calendar are at odds. The more you keep one, the harder it is to keep the other. Advent is definitely lost if the sights and sounds of Christmas ("the holidays") push it off the calendar. And the Christmas season can be lost if we're already tired of it when it arrives.

Maybe it will help to think about the basic good that may underlie even the commercial calendar: a wonderful human desire for festivity, especially in winter. We can try to identify and then put aside the worst aspects of the commercial calendar. We can rejoice in a winter festival that is about far more than spending money.

Christmas Day isn't a deadline. Some people find that January rather than December is a less hectic month for writing cards and for the other things people often do in December. Think about it. You're just as happy to hear from folks one month as another, aren't you? And isn't it better to have get-togethers when folks have time to enjoy them?

Three ways to keep a calmer Advent and a richer Christmas:

1. Resolve to keep Advent, then Christmastime, not the "holiday season." The "holiday season" overstuffs November and December and then leaves January desolate. The preparatory bustle (the shopping, baking and housecleaning) occurs at the same time as the concerts, pageants and parties. No wonder we get stressed out!

Sensibly, the church calendar separates the preparation from the celebration. We rehearse during Advent and have the concert during Christmastime. We clean the house during Advent and throw the party during Christmastime. We bake cookies during Advent and wait to eat them until Christmastime.

2. Leave Advent as free as possible, but plan special events for Christmastime. In Advent most of us need nights home, not nights out. Our skills at saying a gracious "no" will come in handy. Try, if you can, to shift parties, concerts and other enjoyable responsibilities off Advent's calendar and onto Christmastime's. You'll be doing everyone a favor.

Even harder than holding off on Christmas during Advent is celebrating during Christmastime, when so much in our society announces that "the holidays" are over. Put extra effort into planning Christmastime.

In everything, aim the activities at those most likely to feel left out. Christmas is for children, so they say, but it's also for teens, adults and seniors.

In the years after the death of her parents and then her divorce, a woman began to keep several of the Twelve Days of Christmas by inviting over folks who were alone like herself. She doesn't do everything but instead assigns tasks at the time people accept the invitation. That way everyone has a stake in the celebration. She always words her invitations, "Come and be part of my family."

A Christmas custom that really deserves to wait until the last minute is decking the halls with fresh greens and flowers. Their beauty and aroma transform a home. They've just got to be at their fragrant best on Christmas morning!

Poinsettias are native to Central America. Christmas cactuses are native to the Andes. The folklore surrounding mistletoe is European, but a species of this parasitic plant lives in the American South. Amaryllises originated in Africa. Azaleas are mostly from Asia. "English" holly grows wild from Ireland to Armenia, and America has its native hollies, too.

Christmas plants can challenge us to seek the full flowering of the prophet Isaiah's strong words: "As a garden brings forth what is sown, so the Lord will bring forth justice from among the nations."

3. Recognize how Christmas customs, including the get-togethers and music-making, can help us welcome Christ to our homes and to our world. Maybe all we need is a new way of looking at the good old customs. For instance, caroling can be door-to-door hospitality. Mistletoe can be like Noah's olive branch, a sign of peace and reconciliation. Sending cards and giving gifts and enjoying one another's company also can be signs of peace, small but significant ways we make the world ready for Christ.

We received these traditions from Christian people who were steeped in scripture. The Bible's characters were like next-door neighbors to them. Developing this kind of familiarity and then blending it with a wholesome imagination will help us appreciate for ourselves what our ancestors have handed on to us.

The word "tradition" means "hand-me-down." Like any hand-me-down, sometimes a tradition needs alteration to make it fit. We try to fit the needs of our household and also the demands of the gospel.

For instance, our Christian ancestors have handed on to us the custom of using light to celebrate the birth of the Lord. To adapt this tradition to our own hectic schedules, perhaps the outdoor Christmas lights are put up whenever we find the time during Advent, but we wait until Christmas Eve to light them for the first time rather than lighting them as soon as they're up. That way we keep Advent as a time of anticipation. And then as Advent turns into Christmas, we create a great outpouring of light in celebration of our faith.

Traditions may be good, but it's not good if one member of the family gets stuck with the work. And the forethought and fretting that goes into Christmas can be the hardest work of all. Let's share the load fairly. After all, we are one body in Christ.

O Christmas Tree!

What a crazy thing to do! We cut down a tree, drag it indoors, stand it up straight, electrify it, and then hang all sorts of doodads on it. The Europeans who first thought up this notion also decorated trees for Easter, births, weddings, funerals, and many other turning points of life. What were they thinking?

Some folks imagined how a tree can be an emblem of paradise — our first home and, God willing, our final one. Setting up a "paradise tree" seems a grand way to celebrate any homecoming, any gathering of kith and kin.

Is it any wonder that the most old-fashioned tree ornament is the apple?

In Latin the word "apple" is *malus.*

The word "evil" is *malum.* The book of Genesis doesn't tell us what species the forbidden fruit was, but people made of these Latin words a pun and thought that apples hung on Eden's tree of knowledge.

It would be hard to look honestly at ourselves after reading any day's newspapers and deny the presence of evil. The Genesis story ponders this when it tells us that long ago in paradise we ate the forbidden fruit. The home called paradise was left behind, and, ever since, evil and hardship and death have been traveling with us. But they are not the whole story either. We proclaim that Jesus brings us a new and full life. His own "tree" — the holy cross — can be a sign for us that a garden beyond the old paradise is our journey's end.

A Pennsylvania Dutch custom is to decorate the tree with all sorts of dried fruits — strung into clusters or short garlands with the help of strong coat thread and a fat carpet needle.

Did you know that stale popcorn is less brittle and easier to string than freshly popped corn? "Coat thread" is extra-strong and perfect for stringing garlands.

If not bruised or cut, apples may last a few weeks on your Christmas tree. Find some with sturdy stems, and fix them to the tree with yarn tied to the stems. The small variety called "lady apples" are especially beautiful on a tree.

> The tree of life my soul hath seen,
> Laden with fruit, and always green:
> The trees of nature fruitless be;
> Compared with Christ the apple tree.
>
> I'm weary with my former toil;
> Here I will sit and rest awhile:
> Under the shadow I will be
> Of Jesus Christ the apple tree.
>
> This fruit doth make my soul to thrive;
> It keeps my dying faith alive,
> Which makes my soul in haste to be
> With Jesus Christ the apple tree.

These lovely words are from Joshua Smith's collection, *Divine Hymns and Spiritual Songs*, published in New Hampshire in 1784. The words fit the melody of the English folksong "The water is wide" (found in most hymnals under the name "O waly waly"). They also fit the carol "What star is this?" (*"Puer nobis nascitur"*).

Take a winter walk to look at the trees in your neighborhood. Which are biggest? Which have the most interesting shapes? Can you tell one kind from another?

Considering how highly we regard trees at this season, perhaps someone on your gift list can use a book about trees, a guide to identifying trees, membership in a local arboretum, or even a gift certificate from a nursery for purchasing and planting a tree at the right season in your climate.

Did you know that the word "true" has the same root-sound in its Anglo-Saxon origins as our word "tree"? Think how both words mean

> Use toothpicks to stick together prunes, raisins and apricots to form little animals, birds and people. On "take-down-the-tree day" the fruits can be washed and then cooked with lemon and honey into jams and compotes to offer a sweet farewell to your homecoming in paradise.

"something solid and deeply rooted." Trees have their roots in the soil and their branches in the sky. That's why Christians use them as emblems of the joining of earth and heaven.

Here are a few tips for hanging tree lights:
With miniature lights, some people wear rubber gloves and work with the sets plugged in. That way if a set flickers or fails, it's easier to spot the cause. To avoid breakage with large-bulb light sets, remove the bulbs, position the strands on the tree, and then put the bulbs back.

No matter what size light you're using, with each strand, first make sure the plug is near the outlet. (Of course!) Then, starting near the trunk, loop the strand in loose spirals out a branch to the very tip, then back down the same branch to the trunk, and then out another branch, and so on. Why? It's more attractive if strands run in and out like this instead of jumping from branch tip to branch tip.

Did you know that most light sets have tiny fuses in the plugs? You can blow the fuses if you string too many sets together. Don't load onto one plug more than 300 miniature lights or 50 large lights.

What about using a rooted tree that you can plant outside after Christmastime? It's tricky. If you keep the tree more than a few days in a warm room, it will come out of winter dormancy and then freeze dead once it's put outside. Also, if you live where the soil freezes, you won't be able to plant the tree until a thaw. You can dig the hole in autumn, cover it with boards or fill it with leaves, and store the loose soil in a frost-free location.

If you're going to use a rooted tree, pick a species that can survive in your climate. And be sure to plant it where it has enough room to grow.

> *It is poor psychology to anticipate Christmas, to break up the great climax into all kinds of little climaxes, until on the feast itself we are bored and tired of it all, even of the tree if lighted prematurely for small occasions instead of being a sudden, symbolic revelation of the fullness of light in the Holy Night.*
>
> *—Therese Mueller*

There's no substitute for a sturdy tree stand of the right dimensions. Especially if a tree is large, it's more likely to stand straight if the bottom cut is perfectly perpendicular to the trunk. If the tree was frozen when you brought it in, you might need to readjust it in its stand after it thaws out.

Just to be on the safe side (especially if there's a feisty cat in your home), you might be able to wire the tree to a bolt securely anchored in the ceiling or wall.

Try to bring the tree inside as close to Christmas as possible.

That way it's still at its fragrant best from Christmas to Epiphany. Hanging ornaments can be the perfect way to spend Christmas Eve. Do yourself a favor: Wait at least a day after standing the tree up indoors before decorating it. The branches will have time to relax, and so will you!

In most homes setting up the tree involves three stages that probably should be kept separate, perhaps by doing each on a different day. First, the tree itself is carried in and set up. This is hard work and makes a mess. Second, the lights are put on the branches.

Then comes the unpacking and hanging of the ornaments and, in some homes, the making of new ones. The ornamenting of the tree is best done calmly, with plenty of time for relaxation and reminiscing.

No matter when the tree is decorated, it's best lighted on the night of December 24. That way this shining moment—customarily accompanied with plenty of oohing and aahing—becomes a great burst of light to welcome the birth of the Lord.

Your Christmas tree can be more than a beautiful decoration. It can be a spark to praise, a vision of glory, a holy sign of the coming of the reign of God. Your tree can be used to full advantage as the centerpiece of prayerful ritual.

A real tree requires daily watering. Sometimes

this means twice daily. There's no evidence that anything but plain water—no aspirin, pennies or special concoctions— helps a cut tree last longer, but a few drops of bleach added to the water will keep microbial life from fouling it.

When giving your tree its daily drink, give thanks to God for the water, the tree, the day, and for this happy

Blessing of the Tree

God of Adam and Eve,
God of all our ancestors,
we praise you for this tree.
It stirs a memory of paradise,
and brings a foretaste of heaven.

Send your Child,
the flower of the root of Jesse,
to restore your good earth
to the freshness of creation.

Then every tree of the forest
will clap its hands,
and all creation will bless you
from these shining branches.

All glory be yours,
now and for ever. Amen.

season. Give thanks for the water of baptism that brings us new birth.

Each night from Christmas to Epiphany (and then some), the tree is lighted anew. Maybe that just means a flick of a switch, but let your heart leap up each night at the dazzle. As an old carol runs, "All out of darkness we have light, which makes the angels sing this night!"

The lovely light of your Christmas tree is a fitting atmosphere for retelling family stories, for sharing private hopes and fears, for playing games, and for singing and playing carols and other music of the season.

Eventually there comes the day to bid the tree farewell. The Scandinavians have a grand custom for this task, making it one of the jolliest of the year. They call it *Julgransplundring,* the great Christmas plundering! It takes place midway between Christmas Day and Candlemas. At a given signal everyone rushes up to the tree and grabs its edible ornaments. All through Christmastime these decorations—candies, cookies, nuts and fruits—had been "forbidden fruit." But on this day it's as if we are being invited to have our fill of Eden's bounty.

Once the tree is denuded of its other ornaments, the custom is to "waltz Christmas outside." This often turns into a free-for-all, with the tree getting thrown out the highest window, then carried back into the house, back upstairs and back out the window: Christmas is too beloved to leave without protest. Of course there's an awful mess, but the home gets filled with the tree's fragrance, its final blessing.

If there's any life left in it, the tree can be set up outdoors as a winter bird sanctuary. Birds really do benefit from evergreen roosting sites. Some families strip the branches and turn the trunk into a Lenten cross. Be sure to fill a pretty bowl with some of the needles. That way you can inhale an aromatic reminder of Christmas past for several more days.

Do you know folks who would love to have some sort of tree but cannot manage to do that themselves? With their agreement, setting up and then taking down a Christmas tree for them might be the best gift of all.

Peter Mazar

Author's Christmas tree

O Christmas tree,
O Christmas tree,
How lovely God has made you!
Not only green when summer's here,
But in the coldest time of year!
O Christmas tree,
O Christmas tree,
How lovely God has made you!

O Christmas tree,
O Christmas tree,
Your branches shine so brightly!
For in a time of snow and ice,
You lead us into paradise.
O Christmas tree,
O Christmas tree,
Your branches shine so brightly!

Then let the trees of the forest sing
before the coming of the Lord,
who comes to judge the nations,
to set the earth aright,
restoring the world to order.

—Psalm 96:12–13

SPRUCES are wonderfully shaped trees with short needles like fir trees, but the needles are very sharp. Keep them out of carpets! And be warned: If all the needles ever fell off one of your Christmas trees, it probably was a spruce!

PINES make good houseguests because they usually don't shed their long, lovely needles.

White pines have beautiful soft needles in bundles of five, but the branches are weak.

Scotch pines have stiff needles in bundles of two or three, but often have crooked trunks.

FIRS have short, flat, fragrant needles that aren't very sharp. They also hold up well indoors.

Balsam firs have a great aroma! They're used to make most Christmas wreaths.

Douglas firs have medium-length needles.

Fraser firs have short, almost blue needles. They cost more than most other kinds but last the longest.

Be sure your tree is fresh when you buy it. Nothing you can do will resuscitate a dry tree.

Driving a long distance or at high speed with the tree tied to the top of the car can give the tree a wind-burn. Wrap it in a tarp.

Store the tree outdoors in a cold, shady spot until the time to bring it in. Just when you're ready to bring it inside, cut a few inches off the bottom of the trunk. A jagged-tooth saw works well. Never, ever let the cut dry out. If you don't keep the base of the trunk in water, the sap quickly dries and seals the cut from being able to take up water.

'Tis the Gift to Be Simple

Why did gift-giving become so important to Christmas? Of course, there's the gospel story, Matthew 2:1–12, about the Magi who gave the newborn Christ gifts of gold, frankincense and myrrh. We tell this gospel at Epiphany, which is "gift-giving day" for many Christians around the world. Perhaps by giving gifts we're saying that we recognize Christ in others.

Poets of the early church described the mystery of the incarnation as the *sacrum commercium*, the "holy exchange" in which, as Augustine put it, "God becomes human so that humans might become God." Exchanging gifts can be a celebration of the "holy exchange."

Gift-giving is likely to be the seasonal custom that requires the most time and forethought.

The custom sometimes makes all others pale in comparison. As a visitor to the United States said, "Of course I'm homesick. Here you just have presents. In my country we have *Christmas*."

In your home, if you took gift-giving away, would you be taking Christmas away? Imagine Christmas without this custom. Would it be a better and more Christian celebration? This wonderful and powerful custom needs to be kept in scale with everything else.

Some families may want to abandon gift-giving entirely. They don't want a religious festival turned into a swap meet. Many people say when asked what they want for Christmas, "I would like your love," or, "your time," rather than a material gift. We can take them at their word.

Some years we have critical obligations that prevent us from buying or making gifts. Some years we're strapped for money. Do our expectations about giving and receiving adjust to years like that?

Gifts generate a lot of feelings, good and bad.

Talk these over. You just might come closer this season. Because spouses may have grown up with different customs, they especially need to work toward an understanding of what really matters when it comes to gift-giving.

Adults often are more easygoing than children when it comes to changing expectations. Be patient. Any changes can evolve in little ways over the years.

As long as a family can come to a mutual agreement (which means any discussion had better take place months before Christmas), there are all sorts of creative ways to "own" the custom of gift-giving instead of it owning us.

You might decide to limit gifts to small surprises, to stocking-stuffers, to gifts of the sillier sort. Some give only handmade gifts or gifts of volunteer time or gifts given to charity in someone's name. Some households agree to restrict gift-giving just to the children in the family. (That's more or less been the ordinary practice generations ago.)

Everyone can make a point to shop responsibly. We can stick to budgets. We can try to make sure our purchases are socially and environmentally responsible. We can try to make our purchases a gift to the community. Nearly every town has organizations that sell gifts made by people with disabilities or that help people lift themselves out of poverty.

Donations to organizations doing good work (from adopting an animal at the zoo to a contribution to Amnesty International) make wonderful gifts for those who really don't need more things. See Gift-giving Resources on page 29.

Consider the gift of time: A teenager can pledge to be sure to eat dinner with the family on a given day each week. A parent can pledge to read the children a bedtime story every Saturday evening. Or perhaps this year the money spent on presents instead goes toward a family vacation. The gift of times of being together—a gift promised and kept—can be the most splendid of all.

There are several other traditions for giving.
We might boil them down to three principles:

1. Keep it simple. Are we brave enough to try a Christmas of simple gifts? If you think your gift-giving (and receiving) has gotten out of hand, do something different and then see what happens.

Inexpensive gifts can be rich in meaning: a pot of herbs, a jar of honey, a lemon studded with cloves, a ball and jacks, a "Jacob's ladder" (a toy made from strips of cloth

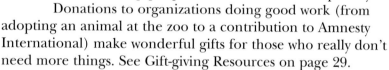
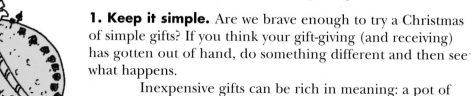

and wooden slats). Such gifts can be as precious as gold and as fragrant as frankincense.

2. Keep it a surprise. A century ago, ads for Christmas gifts might show toys or trinkets, but nothing fancy, because most folks didn't exchange substantial presents. The reason often was more than the constraints of poverty. Even among many of the wealthy it was considered atrocious manners to give something that called too much attention to the giver or that put the receiver under obligation, even the obligation of gratitude.

Maybe we might try this year to give to people who least expect gifts, especially folks in need of consolation or conciliation. Sometimes these gifts can't be wrapped but come in the form of open minds and open arms, in the form of a visit, a long talk, a hug and a kiss.

At the beginning of Advent some families draw names to become someone's secret "Kris Kringle," who performs acts of kindness throughout the season and at Christmas gives a gift. (Although Kris Kringle is now another name for Santa, it originates from the German *Christkindl*, the Christ child.) By drawing names like this everyone in the family becomes involved in choosing gifts.

Maybe the biggest Christmas surprise we can give one another is to take on more roles (or to give up a few) in helping the family keep its Christmas.

3. Think beyond Christmas Day. Epiphany, not Christmas, can be gift-giving day, or you can save the funniest or best gifts to open that day. In some countries January 1 is the day for gifts. New Year's Day and the weekends after Christmas Day (rather than Advent weekends) are great times to gather with relatives and friends to open presents.

In a family where several presents are destined for each person, perhaps each night from Christmas to Epiphany one or two gifts can be opened.

Every generous act of giving, with every perfect gift, is from above, coming down from the Father of lights.
—James 1:17

Gift-giving Resources

These are a few published materials to help us shop more responsibly or more frugally:

Co-op America (a quarterly magazine), 1850 M Street NW, Suite 700, Washington DC 20036; 202-872-5307

Following Christ in a Consumer Society by John Kavanaugh, Orbis Books, 1991

Shopping for a Better World, a booklet by the Council on Economic Priorities, 30 Irving Place, New York NY 10003; 800-729-4237

The Tightwad Gazette by Amy Dacyczyn, Villard Books, 1993

Unplug the Christmas Machine: A Complete Guide to Putting Love and Joy Back into the Season by Jo Robinson and Jean Coppock Staeheli, Quill— William Morrow and Co., 1991

These nonprofit organizations make available gifts that are made by low-income people throughout the world. Artisans receive fair compensation for their work:

Pueblo to People, PO Box 2545, Houston TX 77252-2545; 800-843-5257

SELFHELP Crafts of the World, 704 Main Street, Box 500, Akron PA 17501; 717-859-8100

SERRV International (Sales Exchange for Refugee Rehabilitation Vocations), PO Box 365, New Windsor MD 21776; 800-423-0071

The United Nations International Children's Fund (UNICEF) sells cards and gifts in many locations; call 800-FOR-KIDS. UNICEF has its own "Winter Collection" catalog; call 212-686-5522.

Many people give Christmas gifts by donating money or time in someone's name. The Salvation Army, Catholic Charities and the St. Vincent de Paul Society are worthy local organizations whose addresses and phone numbers can be found in the phone book.

Here are some other national and international organizations that need our help:

Amnesty International USA, 322 Eighth Avenue, New York NY 10001; 212-807-8400

Bread for the World, 1100 Wayne Avenue, Suite 1000, Silver Springs MD 20910; 301-608-2400

Catholic Relief Services, 209 West Fayette Street, Baltimore MD 21201-3443; 800-736-3467

Children's Defense Fund, 25 E Street NW, Washington DC 20001; 202-628-8787

Church World Service, PO Box 968, Elkhart IN 46515; 219-264-3102

Habitat for Humanity International, Habitat and Church Streets, Americus GA 31709-3498; 912-924-6935

Oxfam America, 26 West Street, Boston MA 02111; 617-482-1211

Pax Christi USA, 348 East Tenth Street, Erie PA 16503; 814-453-4955

Bethlehem, the House of Bread

Francis of Assisi had Christmas Mass celebrated in a stable full of animals. At that time, Christians and Muslims were killing each other for control of the Holy Land. This disgusted Francis. In worshiping in a stable, he was saying that any place can be Bethlehem. All the earth is holy land.

Even before there were nativity scenes, there was this custom of turning odd corners of the earth into Bethlehem, especially in the home. Floors were covered with straw. Tables were spread with straw and grain as if they were mangers. Animals were given high honors because, as a church antiphon goes, they were "first to see the Lord." The custom of not eating meat on Christmas and Epiphany Eves can be a sign of respect for furred and feathered creatures.

Folklore says that animals kneel and sing praises at midnight on Christmas Eve: "Heaven and nature sing."

In Hebrew, "Bethlehem" means "house of bread." An old custom for the meals of Christmastime is to begin by sharing a single loaf of bread. Some people's Christmas bread is a wafer, like the bread often used at the eucharist. For others, the Christmas loaf is yeasty and braided and fruit-filled, a sign of unity and fullness. A portion of the bread is fed to pets and farm animals, mailed to distant friends and relatives, and even scattered on the graves of the dead. All things have communion in Christ.

One way to make the home a new Bethlehem

is by setting up a nativity scene. It deserves as much straw, flowers, evergreens and creative effort as we can muster.

Some people make a backdrop showing scenes from their own neighborhood. Some people add new figures each year. Some carve their own figures or craft them in some other way. If you do this, be sure to add figures of your household and its "honorary members," too.

A usual spot for the scene is beneath the Christmas tree. That way the tree with its ornaments becomes the shining universe surrounding Bethlehem, a vision of creation at peace — like Eden. Some folks add family-photo ornaments to the tree as a way to place themselves in paradise.

Barnyard animals welcome the day of Christ's birth by speaking in Latin, each with its own proper animal-accent: Roosters crow, "Christus natus est!" (Christ is born!). Cows bellow, "Ubi?" (Where?). Sheep bleat, "In Bethlehem" (which means the same thing in Latin or English). And donkeys bray, "Eamus!" (Let's go!).

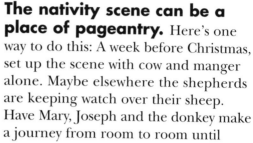

The nativity scene can be a place of pageantry. Here's one way to do this: A week before Christmas, set up the scene with cow and manger alone. Maybe elsewhere the shepherds are keeping watch over their sheep. Have Mary, Joseph and the donkey make a journey from room to room until they arrive in Bethlehem near sundown on Christmas Eve. Then, for a final time as Advent ends, sing "O come, O come, Emmanuel."

By reading Luke 2:1 – 7 and then singing "Silent night," make a simple ceremony of putting the child in the manger late on Christmas Eve or early on Christmas morning. The ceremony can end with hugs and kisses "to welcome Christmas in." What a wonderful way to begin opening presents!

Christmas morning especially is a good time for the angels and shepherds and their lambs to arrive. Read Luke 2:8 – 14 and join in "Hark the herald angels sing."

On Christmas Day or the day after, begin the journey of the Magi and their camels, who follow the star room to room through the home until they arrive in Bethlehem at Epiphany. What night will the Magi rest in your bedroom?

In chapter four of the letter to the Galatians, Saint Paul offers lessons on what it means to be a child of God. He calls God our father and the new Jerusalem our mother! He also uses a parental image that comes close to describing one of the great wonders we celebrate at Christmas: "My children! I will go through the pains of giving birth over and over again until Christ is formed in you."

Mary and Joseph, Elizabeth and Zachary, Anna and Simeon—these are the lowly, the poor, the meek. Psalm 37 says they will own the earth and delight in peace. Psalm 149 tells us that God will adorn them with victory. Read Zephaniah 3:12 – 20. What lovely words!

Lord Jesus has the last word: See Luke 6:20 – 38. Who are the least, the left-out, the oppressed, the forgotten of our own day and age?

Some folks set up a miniature village underneath the Christmas tree or elsewhere in the home. People used to make the scene look like their own neighborhood, populated with the folks they knew going about their daily business. In the middle was the nativity scene. Christ is born among us! These old-time nativity scenes may look quaint to us nowadays but were not old-fashioned to their creators. Instead of trying to re-create the long ago and far away, the scenes were set up to offer insight into the here-and-now.

The scenes sometimes poke fun at the local goings-on: kids playing pranks, neighbors quarrelling, someone drunk, someone tampering with a grocer's scale or stealing fruit. In the middle of this sinful world, Christ is born.

Imagine Christ being born down the block from you, maybe next door, perhaps even in your own home. That's how Christmas is best understood.

Blessing of a Nativity Scene

*Bless us, Lord,
as we come to Bethlehem,
where animals and angels,
shepherds and seekers
together behold your face.*

*Here snow becomes straw
and frost becomes flowers,
as winter melts into everlasting spring.*

*In our holy Christmas,
give us the riches of your poverty.
Show us the wonder of simplicity
as we join with the angels
in singing your praise:
Glory in heaven and peace on earth,
now and for ever. Amen.*

Hannah and Samuel

Sarah and Isaac

A nativity scene is a holy shrine, a place to pray every day of the season. Each encounter with the scene can be a time for

A psalm

A short scripture reading

Petitions to God

The Lord's Prayer

The sign of peace (embrace each other)

And of course, sing carols! "Joy to the world" is a version of Psalm 98 that everyone knows.

The birth of Jesus is one of many nativity stories in the Bible. Take some time this season to get acquainted with some of these tales:

Hagar and Ishmael

Hagar and Ishmael, Genesis 16:1–16
Sarah and Isaac, Genesis 18:1–15; 21:1–8
Rebekah and her twins, Genesis 25:19–34
Moses and his mother, Exodus 2:1–10
Manoah's wife and Samson, Judges 13:2–24
Hannah and Samuel, 1 Samuel 1:1—2:11
Elizabeth and John, Luke 1:5–25, 57–80

How are these stories alike, and how are they different? And while you're telling nativity stories, be sure to tell your own family stories about births and other beginnings.

Rebekah & her twins

It's customary to keep the scene up until February 2, Candlemas. On Candlemas Eve tuck a few of the first flowers of spring into the straw (even if these have to be coaxed into bloom by you or a florist). On Candlemas Day dismantle the scene. You might put its straw and dried greens in an outdoor barbecue and make a great, brief blaze to bid Christmas farewell.

In These Twelve Days Let Us Be Glad!

Some people are surprised to find out that the Twelve Days of Christmas come after Christmas Day. The French and English counted those days from December 26 to January 6. Other Europeans usually began the count on Christmas Day itself, making January 6 the "thirteenth day." Both counts give us a baker's dozen of days from December 25 to January 6 for passing over from the old year to the new.

Nowadays we think of the new year beginning as the clock chimes midnight between December 31 and January 1. In the old days the turning of the year was considered more of a process than a moment in time. That's a wonderful way to think of the Twelve Days: Fast away the old year passes! Hail the new, ye lads and lasses! Fa-la-la-la-la . . .

Beginnings and endings are mystical junctures. When two times butt up against each other, perhaps eternity seeps out through the crack. That kind of thinking is a reason people imagined that the Twelve Days are especially good for reminiscing and for sharing hopes. Take some time each evening to do just that.

The Twelve Days have a beginning (Christmas Day), a middle (New Year's Day) and an end (Epiphany). All Twelve Days are part of Christmas, but certain days have special names:

December 26, Saint Stephen's Day. Today is also called "Boxing Day," and the name has nothing to do with sports. People handed out

It's no wonder that round things — such as wreaths and coiled breads and circle-dances (which is what the word "carol" once meant) — were thought perfect for Christmastime, as well as for other beginnings and endings in life, such as births, weddings and funerals. At those times especially we enter into the mystery of heaven's timelessness.

Most of those customs have slipped away, but a few remain. Think about this when you cut into a minced pie, or encircle your brow with a silly hat, or hold hands around a table.

Christian tradition says that Christmas is a birth, a wedding, even a funeral. Christ is born, heaven and earth are wed, death itself has died! Our keeping the circle of the seasons can be the "wedding band" we wear to remind ourselves and others of our fidelity to Christ in a love that even death cannot part.

Saint Stephen

"Saint Stephen's almsboxes" of food and clothing to those in need. The gifts were gathered all through Advent. Maybe this is the best day of the year for writing a check to charity. It's also a good day for giving a treat to postal and sanitation workers.

Deacon Stephen's job was to distribute the belongings of the church fairly among its members. He was murdered for his faith. The name "Stephen" means "leafy crown," like the laurel wreaths athletes received, or like the circle of evergreens that might be hanging on your front door. It's a Christian symbol of martyrdom, a word that means "to give witness."

I have fought the good fight, I have finished the race, I have kept the faith. From now on there is reserved for me the leafy crown of justice, which the Lord, the just judge, will give me on that day, and not only to me but also to those who have longed for his appearing.
— 2 Timothy 4:7 – 8

Another way to give witness to Christ is to go caroling. Bring hospitality door to door. Who could use an earful or a whole boxful of Christmas cheer? On this "feast of Stephen" Good King Wenceslas knows that "ye who now will bless the poor, shall yourselves find blessing."

This carol is easy to sing as a round, like "Row, row, row your boat." Divide into two groups. Group one starts singing. Group two starts at the beginning just as group one gets to the beginning of the second line. (So group two is singing "Good" just as group one is singing "on.") Try singing it that way. It's fun!

December 27, St. John's Day. Custom identifies John, one of the twelve apostles, with the "beloved disciple" of the gospel according to John. One of the scripture readings today is the Easter story from that gospel: The beloved disciple runs to Jesus' tomb, looks into the empty tomb and believes.

*Good King Wenceslas looked out
on the feast of Stephen,
when the snow lay round about,
deep and crisp and even:
Brightly shone the moon that night,
though the frost was cruel,
when a poor man came in sight,
gath'ring winter fuel.*

*"Hither, page, and stand by me;
if thou know'st it, telling,
yonder peasant, who is he?
Where and what his dwelling?"
"Sire, he lives a good league hence,
underneath the mountain,
right against the forest fence
by Saint Agnes' fountain."*

*"Bring me flesh, and bring me wine,
bring me pine logs hither:
Thou and I will see him dine,
when we bear them thither."
Page and monarch, forth they went,
forth they went together
through the rude wind's wild lament
and the bitter weather.*

*"Sire, the night is darker now,
and the wind blows stronger;
fails my heart, I know not how;
I can go no longer."
"Mark my footsteps, good my page!
Tread thou in them boldly:
Thou shalt find the winter's rage
freeze thy blood less coldly."*

*In his master's steps he trod,
where the snow lay dinted.
Heat was in the very sod
which the saint had printed!
Therefore, Christian folk, be sure,
wealth or rank possessing,
ye who now will bless the poor,
shall yourselves find blessing.*

Not surprisingly, there's a lot of Easter in every Christmas.

It's an old custom this night to drink a toast "to the love of good Saint John!" In John's gospel Jesus calls himself the vine and his followers the branches. The feast became a vine-growers' holiday because of a legend that John drank poisoned wine without harm. Maybe we need a day every Christmastime to focus on the holy pleasures and the terrible perils of alcohol.

December 28, Holy Innocents' Day.
You won't hear the gospel about the holy innocents in church on Sundays, so tell it today: Matthew 2:13–23.

The Play of Herod was a must-see every Christmastime in the Middle Ages. As in the gospel story, the wicked old king spits and fumes that the Magi deceived him. In a rage, he slaughters the children. Their mothers wail, and you think that this is how the awesome and terrifying story is going to end.

But no. Gabriel descends with the whole company of heaven singing *Te Deum laudamus*, "We praise you, O God." The murdered children rise up and sing with the angels. Their tearful mothers sing. Mary and Joseph sing. The Magi come back on stage and sing. The audience sings. Even rotten old Herod joins in praising God.

In today's feast we proclaim that when our year dwindles down, when time itself will stop, Christ will call all creation to rise together in praise.

Considering all the suffering we inflict on children, we have good reasons for leaving the Christmas lights off today, for fasting, for laying low. Every generation has its Herods who begrudge the coming generation its existence. Rachel will never cease her weeping.

That's one aspect of this day. But there's also the *Te Deum*, the against-all-odds defiance of death. Even our sorrows get drawn into the Christmas mystery. As a carol tells us, "All out of darkness we have light."

Today also is called "Childermas" (the "childer" are the innocents), and it became a feast day for every child, innocent or not. (On this day they get the benefit of the doubt.) Zoos and planetariums are good places to take children this season; it just wouldn't be Christmas without animals and stars.

December 31, New Year's Eve. The last day of the year is Saint Sylvester's Day. He was a fourth-century pope who said that for Christians all days are holy. If we live with an eye to eternity, every day can be a feast.

According to folklore, after Sylvester died he received the keys to heaven's clock and was put in charge of shepherding earth's annual circuit around the sun. His bishop's crook was transformed into a scythe so he could harvest God's children into heaven. Now we call him "Father Time." In Europe, New Year revelers are still called "sylvesters."

Don't sit inside staring at TV to tell when it's midnight. Wear a watch and step outside with bells and horns in hand. The fresh air will do you good, and if you live in town, the booms and beeps at midnight will thrill you.

Go a little crazy at midnight. Go crazy enough to forget old wrongs, to hug neighbors, to make such a joyful noise that winter, death and the devil are frightened into oblivion. Making a racket at midnight is an act of kindness, because according to Luke 12:35 – 40, no one should be caught asleep when the master returns.

New Year's Eve is a little like the end of the world. There's an awesomeness and power to this night that we might lose if we mask it with intoxicants. Some people make sure to take

go to page 41

Make a gingerbread house without gingerbread: Cut doors and windows out of a small, square box. Cover the window openings with cellophane. Add a cardboard roof and maybe a chimney. Use the box as a frame and "glue" cookies or graham crackers to it using tubes of cake icing. Add candies and frosting.

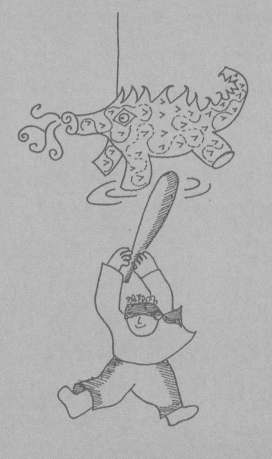

Christmastime is for party games, from piñatas to Parcheesi. Did you know that "pin the tail on the donkey" was originally for Yuletide? In the old days when they played this game, the kindly (and tailless) animal that carried the Holy Family to Egypt was more likely to be a person than a poster—a moving target! Ouch!

You might put a new board game under the tree to unwrap during Christmastime. Or haul out and rediscover the games that got tossed into a closet over the years.

Here's an idea that's for the birds: Outdoors, decorate a tree with edible ornaments made out of berries, orange peels, apple slices, suet, popcorn, cracked corn and other grains. (Don't use anything dangerous to wildlife, such as thread, hooks or plastic rings.) Most hardware stores sell birdseed and feeding stations. Different species require different foods and even different feeders.

Any kind of small, living tree may work, or you can wire a cut Christmas tree to a stake driven into the ground. Birds benefit from such evergreen perches especially during winter storms.

If you set up a feeding station, keep it stocked all winter. Birds come to depend on it; it may take a few weeks for them to discover it, so be patient.

On a windless night fill the yard with lit birthday candles for a few moments of magic. It's extra beautiful (and extra safe) after a snowfall.

Feeling cranky? Or blue? Or maybe you've eaten too much? Take a walk. Open your eyes and ears to winter. There's an amazing amount of life around us. Believe it or not, this is when cardinals begin their spring songs. Maybe there's a first snowdrop or some winter-blooming heath in evidence. Surely there are Christmas lights to enjoy at night.

An early morning walk has its rewards: Before dawn on January 3 and 4 comes the finest meteor shower of the year.

The worse the weather, the better it is to get outdoors. So what if your nose drips and cheeks get ruddy? Make hot chocolate when you get home and stir it with a candy cane.

a quiet walk sometime this night, even if it's just a respite from the fun. Reflect on the mystery of the arrival of Christ, of the passage of time, of the old made new.

> **So take my hand, my trusty friend,**
> **and gi' us a hand o' thine!**
> **We'll drink a right good willie-waught**
> **for auld lang syne.**
> **For auld lang syne, my dear, for auld lang syne,**
> **We'll take a cup o' kindness yet**
> **for auld lang syne.**

This is the second verse of Bobbie Burns' song. Auld lang syne means "old long since," a Scottish way of saying "the good old days."

January 1, New Year's Day. Almost everywhere it's customary to try to live this day the way we'd like to live all year long. That's why it's very bad luck to shop on New Year's Day (it portends a spendthrift year) and very good luck to visit relatives and neighbors. New Year's is an open-house occasion. Sing "Deck the halls" and you'll catch the spirit!

A great custom is to leave sweet surprises on the doorsteps of neighbors. As a Yankee proverb puts it, "Begin the new year square with everyone." Or, in the words of this old carol set to the tune of "Greensleeves":

> **And so with New Year gifts each friend**
> **unto each other they do send.**
> **God grant we may our lives amend**
> **and that the truth may appear!**
> **Now, like the snake, our skin**
> **cast off of evil thoughts and sin,**
> **and so the year begin:**
> **God send us a merry new year!**

On this day the church celebrates Mary as the *theotokos*, a Greek word meaning "God-bearer." Saint Cyril, a bishop of Jerusalem in the fourth century, used this title for all people who share the body and blood of Christ.

Today's gospel reading is Luke 2:15–21. It takes up where we left off on Christmas night. It's almost a blueprint for keeping the Christmas spirit alive with reflection,

We know that aromas can stir up the memory in amazing ways. Making a favorite childhood recipe for someone may be an effective (and certainly is the most delicious) way to conjure up recollections.

peacemaking and hearty praise. We hear that the shepherds start to sing the song of the angels. The peace of heaven begins to take hold on earth. The shepherds spread the astonishing news that Christ is among us. And then we hear that "Mary treasured all these words and pondered them in her heart."

New Year's Day is a great day for treasuring your own family histories, and it's not too hard to mastermind some reminiscing: Invite family and friends, but also invite a few strangers because they help us mind our manners. Also, it can be more fun to tell the family stories to folks who never heard them before. And who knows? Some strangers may even introduce the spark of romance to the storytelling!

Bring out the family albums and other memorabilia. Fill the room with candles and quiet carols. Then let the teaching and learning that is so important to storytelling begin. There's only one taboo: Avoid electronic interference in the form of television and telephones! And although there's a time and place for cameras, this is not one of them.

What's so magical about such storytelling is that by recollecting memories of the past, we're making memories for the future. Sometimes reminiscing takes a few ice-breakers, and New Year's Day is filled with customary games.

One is to pour a beaten egg or hot wax into cold water. The weird shapes that form are supposed to jog memories and prognosticate the future. Another game is to crack walnuts or pecans and allow their curves (and maybe even their worminess) to inspire the imagination.

A fun custom is to peel an apple or orange in a single spiral strip. (Don't slip or the charm is broken.) Toss the peel backwards over a shoulder. What letter does it form? That letter, so the folklore goes, somehow is important to your past or your future. What can it mean?

The Epíphany of the Lord

It's Epiphany! So what if "Epiphany" is hard to pronounce? When you say this word, you're saying a mouthful. It means "appearing," "manifesting," "revealing." The scriptures sometimes use this wondrous word to mean that incredible time-outside-time when Christ will appear in glory.

The coming of this mighty day has been troubling the church all through Advent, and surely such a day is worth fretting over. But now, at Epiphany, we put troubles aside and welcome the day with a whoop and a holler: Come, Lord Jesus!

Because this day gets us ready for the Last Day, Epiphany traditions are chock-full of hospitality, generousness and imagination. We want to be numbered with those who recognize Christ in their sisters and brothers. We take our cue from the Magi, who went to great lengths to meet the Lord.

Some people say that Epiphany marks the end of the Christmas season. But that doesn't quite square with long-standing tradition. Epiphany is too jolly a day for such a bittersweet activity as bidding Christmas farewell. (We have Candlemas, February 2, for saying our goodbyes.)

A Danish proverb says that Christmas remains in the home as long as there is hospitality to guests and outgoing kindness to strangers. So let's keep Christmas as long as we can! In the march of seasons, Epiphany can be the grand finale and the even grander beginning to a new year of grace.

On this merriest day of our merry Christmas,

the church colors everything in superlatives—even the scriptures. Not one but three gospel stories are told at Epiphany: the visit of the Magi (Matthew 2:1–12), the Lord's baptism in the River Jordan (Mark 1:9–11), and the wedding feast at Cana (John 2:1–11).

This is the day that stars and clouds, wine and water, rivers and skies—every blessed thing in the universe—cries out the good news: Jesus Christ is Lord!

No wonder the church sings this giddy and deliciously confusing antiphon at Epiphany, one that mixes all three gospel stories:

go to page 45

Epiphany is decidedly rich in customs worth returning year after year. We'll take a look at three that can be combined into a single ceremony— serving the Twelfth Night cake, choosing the Epiphany monarch, and the blessing of the home.

We don't choose the Epiphany queen or king as much as we discover her or his identity among us. One way to do that requires some sort of Christmasy cake. Fruitcake or minced pie is traditional, but any round confection will do, even angel food or a bundt cake.

Some folks decorate the cake with gumdrop or candied fruit "jewels." The circular shape conjures up an image of a crown, or the new year, or even eternity. Fruits and spices are meant to remind us of the gifts of the Magi.

At dessert time before serving the cake, cut it evenly into as many pieces as you have guests. In one piece hide a coin or bean or—as they do in New Orleans—a tiny figure of the infant Jesus. We're searching for Christ today, aren't we?

Whoever finds this token (chew carefully!) is crowned, robed, saluted and kissed. So you'll need a crown (a party hat?), royal robes (a quilt, or maybe the Sunday comics taped together), and, of course, plenty of noise-makers. Remember New Year's midnight? The salute can be even more raucous.

The newly crowned royal personage has three official duties. (Fame always comes with a price tag.) First, a toast must be offered for a happy, healthy new year. Second, the house must be blessed. Third, some time before Ash Wednesday the monarch has the responsibility to host the Carnival party. One celebration deserves another.

$$19 + C + M + B + 99$$

**Today the Bridegroom claims his bride,
the Church,
since Christ has washed her sins away
in Jordan's waters;
the Magi hasten with their gifts
to the royal wedding;
and the wedding guests rejoice,
for Christ has changed water into wine.
Alleluia!**

There's Epiphany for you: a royal wedding! Advent was the courtship, Christmas Day the exchange of vows. Now it's time for dining and dancing and, ah yes, the wedding night. What a day! It's like a wedding and it's like the end of the world!

Although Epiphany is now kept on the first Sunday after New Year's Day, its ancient day is January 6.
In the course of the year, that day more or less marks the beginning of earlier and earlier sunrises now that the winter solstice has passed. By January 6 we can notice that the sun sets later than it did in December. We have taken our first steps to springtime!

An Epiphany hymn praises this renewal of the sun, an image of Christ the Lord:

**Brightest and best of the suns of the morning,
dawn on our darkness and lend us thine aid!
Star of the east, the horizon adorning,
guide where our infant Redeemer is laid.**

Celebrating Epiphany offers an opportunity and a challenge.
The challenge is in keeping a festival when so many around us are packing it away. Create a festival from scratch, a homemade holiday that may not have commercial support but that does have centuries of Christian tradition to fill it with beauty and power.

We know what it takes to make a festival day — good company, good food, good song. No doubt the house is still filled with the signs of the season. (You certainly don't want to take down the Christmas finery until Epiphany is over.) If you

go to page 47

19 + C + M + B + 99

Epiphany is the customary day to bless the home in the new year. Here's a lovely way to do this:

Whether you live alone or with others, gather inside or outside the front door. (Of course, your pets should be there, too.) Perhaps with the aid of a stepstool, write over the door with chalk:

00 + C + M + B + 00

The numerals are those of the new year. C–M–B stand for the legendary names of the Magi—Caspar, Melchior and Balthasar. (Although in some places, such as India, the Magi number 12 or even 70!) The chalk represents human flesh, created by God from clay, and is used as an emblem of the incarnation.

C–M–B also stands for the Latin words *Christus, mansionem benedicat:* "Christ, bless the house." Here's an old rhyme to accompany the blessing:

Caspar, Melchior, Balthasar!
Though the spring seems very far,
    over us has ris'n a star.
Though the cold grows stronger,
    now the days grow longer.
Though the world loves night,
    Christ is born our light.

Some people do this writing over every threshold in the house. That's appropriate in January, a month that literally means "doorway"—our entrance into the year.

Even if you bless just the front door, afterwards everyone walks from room to room sprinkling each room with water, a sign of the River Jordan. Pause in each room to give thanks for the activities that take place there. Hurrah for the kitchen! Hurrah for bathrooms and bedrooms! And hurrah (especially) for the basement furnace!

Pluck a twig from the Christmas tree to use as a water sprinkler. As you go, sing an alleluia or a favorite carol. Joy to the world, the Lord is come!

can't manage a get-together on January 6 or on Epiphany Sunday, then any day early in January will do just fine.

To offer an Epiphany toast to everyone's "wassail" (meaning "good health"), any kind of festive beverage will do. Here's the recipe for an old-time drink called "lamb's wool punch." (The white apple flesh floating in the punch supposedly looks like wool.)

In a big pot, add a container of frozen apple juice concentrate (or frozen lemonade) to a couple of quarts of apple cider. Heat gently and add a stick of unsalted butter, a half cup of brown sugar, and a teaspoonful each of cinnamon, nutmeg and ginger. Drink it hot. You can stud lemon slices with cloves and add these, too.

With a knife, pierce a few small apples straight through to keep them from exploding when heated. In the oven or microwave, roast the apples until they begin to soften. Split and seed them and add them to your hot punch.

Eggnog also makes a fine Epiphany beverage. Why? The baptism of Jesus in the Jordan River is one of the gospels we tell at this season. This event brings to mind a parallel with Jesus' namesake, the Israelite leader Joshua. (The names "Jesus" and "Joshua" are versions of the same name, meaning "Savior.") Like Joshua, Jesus also leads his people through the Jordan River and into the promised land, "a land flowing with milk and honey."

Over the years Christians have celebrated their baptismal entrance into this land by feasting on sweetened dairy products such as eggnog, a deluxe version of milk and honey. Wassail! To your health!

No matter how you celebrate, Epiphany is open-door hospitality, a time to make your home glitter with the exuberance and mystery of gold, frankincense and myrrh.

All of us are kings and queens who have come to adore the Lord. And when we open our door in love to wayfaring strangers and their strange gifts, all of us are members of God's holy family, bound together on this Twelfth Day of Christmas as God's true love.

For the star shines over us, we who have passed through the Jordan of baptism, we who bear the name of Christ!

Carnival:
Feast before the Fast

Between Epiphany and Ash Wednesday comes Carnival, a high-steppin', high calorie antidote to cabin fever. We deserve—no, we *need*—this time to rise from winter darkness into the light of fantasy, imagination and generous hospitality. Round foods (such as pancakes and doughnuts) are customary fare as edible wishes for the sun's return. We use up fattening foods before the Lenten fast. That's how Mardi Gras—the "Greasy Tuesday" before Ash Wednesday—got its name.

Kick up your heels at Carnival! The season is synonymous with the samba and reggae, with the polka and waltz. Winter dancing keeps muscles in tone. It's heart-smart, and it's healthy for the romantic heart, too.

Carnival has gathered to itself a world's worth of folktales. Pinocchio and Petrushka, Cinderella and Sleeping Beauty, Rapunzel and the Pied Piper are tales to be told late into a winter's night. As in many Bible stories, justice and mercy are forerunners of living happily ever after.

To get ready for Lent, we can laugh at our sins at a Carnival masquerade party: The overbearing might wear bear masks, the messy wear pig masks. Horns and pitchfork befit the thoroughly incorrigible.

At midnight on Mardi Gras the masks come off, the dancing stops, and Lent begins, a time to see one another as we truly are. "Lent" is an old word meaning "lengthen" because days rapidly grow longer. Even if the snow is still falling fast in your part of the world, during Lent winter passes over into spring.

To say farewell to winter, indoors you can bash a snowman piñata or outdoors pelt a real one. One family bids old-man-winter adieu by making a snowman out of marshmallows stuck together with toothpicks. He sits atop a fruitcake that's set alight with flaming brandy. When the fire's over, all that's left of winter is a gooey crust on the cake. Literally speaking, winter's licked!